Don't Eat the Scraps

Scraps

and other powerful "Jules' Rules" for Success in Any New Relationship

BY JULES PRICE

Copyright © 2019 Jules Price

Cover and illustrations by Pearly Lim

All rights reserved.

Published by: Listen2Life Marketing

ISBN: 978-0-578-59090-5

ACKNOWLEDGMENTS

I have many people to thank for making this second book a reality. To all my incredible friends—your support and friendship mean the world to me, and I'm a better person by far for having known you. Beth, Rebecca, Marci, Lily, Cyndi, Jen, Savannah, Kari, Jennie, Vanessa, Phebe, Rachel, Jill, Margaretha, Robin C, Heather, Ana, Kara, Kaitlyn, Sheryl, Nicole, Krissy, Paula, Stephanie, Alison, Kaela, Linda T, Jackie, Linda L, Monica, Robin F, Joanne, Leah, Gayle, Mike, Pablo, Johnny B, and of course, Jeremy and Mom. Love you all so much!

We just need more women to understand this concept that I'm about to describe so that we don't misconstrue their intentions, and we can live harmoniously. The more educated we become about the fact that this behavior does in fact occur, the more everyone can go about their merry way!

You may be familiar with the common science fiction thriller concept, as in the movie, "The Butterfly Effect," wherein someone can massively alter the future by going back in time and changing events that have occurred in the past. When this happens, everything ultimately gets completely screwy. People start disappearing out of photos that they used to be in, children never are born, your mother ends up not being your mother, and general mayhem ensues.

Well, it stands to reason that the same dire consequences have the potential to occur now that this top-secret concept is finally and delicately being brought to light.

If men were to become aware of their

own unintended pattern of scrap-flinging behaviors, they would start implementing anywhere from minuscule to dangerously large changes that would ultimately affect the entire balance of this delicate "relationship equation."

In fact, armed with this new alarming knowledge, men's behavior would most certainly morph into some kind of odd and unique strain of the original virus that would be much harder to identify, combat, and eventually eradicate.

Therefore I can't emphasize enough that it's of the utmost importance for all women everywhere to make a pact, though admittedly it may seem extreme: If you see anyone of the male gender reading this book, you MUST (without hesitation) leap forward energetically, grab it out of his unsuspecting hands, shout, "It's for the good of womankind!" and run like a maniac in the opposite direction.

Now in the day and age of e-books, I'm fully aware that this task becomes incredibly more complicated. But in taking a hard line with this, I must suggest that every time you see a male specimen reading any kind of e-book, or even perhaps squinting at his phone (which will ultimately become their only hope), you must peer over his shoulder to see the small print at the top, secure the device, and throw it into the closest water source, if the title of this book reveals itself.

I realize that there are inevitably those who may feel this is a tad bit reactionary, and believe me, I understand your initial reluctance to carry out such an aggressive counter-maneuver. But I will remind you, it has taken years and years for this concept to be formulated and finally be brought to the surface. All it would take is for men to begin to become uber-aware of their actions (because they really do have NO IDEA that they do this), and before we know it, the behavior will spiral and evolve into something more deadly, more sinister, and more complex than ever before.

Even more importantly, all the women

who have up till now been immeasurably helped by finally understanding this issue and being confidently aware of how to navigate the murky, scrap-filled waters, will once again be thrust into darkness, and it may take another 50 years or so before a new cure or workaround is established. I don't have to tell you how detrimental this would be, for all relationships everywhere.

When you think about it, we are protecting the men too, since it all works out for the best on both sides when the scraps are interpreted and navigated properly.

Therefore, I'm sure you'll agree that the benefits of keeping the "Scraps Theory" a world-wide massive secret far outweigh the potential embarrassment of ripping the electronic or hard copies out of their unsuspecting furry hands, and even perhaps braving the occasional arrest for allegations of inflicted stress or property damage against us.

(Note: As long as there is a female police

officer in the vicinity of the station, these charges will simply not stick. Even as we speak, the Scrap Defense is becoming more and more widely embraced in all such reported cases globally.)

So hopefully we can all just agree to stand unified in protecting what we hold dear—and let's move forward!

3—JUST THE SCRAPS, MA'AM

So, what does it all mean? What is all this build-up really about? What are "scraps?" Why shouldn't you eat them? Is this a diet book? How does this relate in any way to dating? And are the first six to eight weeks of any courtship really a critical incubator period that must be treated differently than the rest of the ensuing relationship?

Well hopefully these questions and more will all be answered to your satisfaction, and you can determine for yourself as to whether this makes any sense, rings any bells, and resonates with you. If not, you can fling aside this theory as easily as a low-flying scrap, floating in the breeze.

But if you do connect to what this chapter is all about, it just may save you and some of your informed friends from some impending and easily avoided heartbreaks.

Before I get into the actual theory, it's important to state this caveat. I think by now, in this day and age, we can make two fairly agreed-upon assumptions:

1) That for the most part, men and women do think, feel and operate differently.

2) That there are exceptions to every rule of course, but stereotypes are created for

the sole reason that general patterns of behaviors do in fact tend to emerge.

So please read this section not with a critical eye that wants to pull it all apart and find the one or two individuals you know who absolutely do not do this. *("Humphrey wasn't like that all! He was kind and open and steady from day one!!")*

But instead, approach it with the view that although it may not apply to 100% of the population, there is a very large range of people in whom this very behavior does occur and can therefore be identified and navigated according to the forthcoming outlined theory.

So, are you ready? Here's how it works. Let's get scrap-a-licious.

Have you ever noticed when you're on a first, second or third date with a new, interesting, handsome and definitely a "there-are-real-possibilities-with-this-one" kind of guy, that he starts saying things that are strangely indicative of "future time spent together?" For instance:

"Well, when you meet my brother, you'll see that..."

Or "Oh yes, I always go to Martha's Vineyard in the summer—You'll have to come next year!"

Or, "I'm thinking about going to see Pink Floyd in July. Hey, you should join me!"

Or, "I have a house on Kiawah Island. What are you doing in a few weeks?"

Now before I comment on what's going on here, I want you to look back on those sentences, and VERY CLEARLY imagine yourself saying these things to HIM. Would you ever say those things in the first week, month, or even six months of dating someone? Hell to the no!!

I can very confidently assume that NO woman (because hang on a second—if you're male, then you definitely should never have gotten this far without someone ripping this book from your clutches! Step away from the book and respectfully turn it in to your nearest favorite female with great remorse and an apologetic demeanor). So, I repeat, NO woman would ever say these things anywhere close to the first few months of a relationship.

Don't believe me? Try saying it out loud then. "When you meet my mother..." What?? You just wouldn't do it. Women are socialized to never say anything like that. Ever.

Instead, we are socialized to listen. To look for signs or clues. To be more reserved. To wait and see how it unfolds. To let the other person dictate the pace until we see how things are going. To sit back and see if this relationship might have a future. Right?

Even if you haven't thought about that, you would never, ever say something future-oriented on your first, second, third, or fifteenth date until you have seen signs that things were moving confidently in that direction.

So, here's where the problem comes in. The male gender DOES say these things. And these are called "scraps." Say it with me. Scraps! Little morsels and nuggets of deliciousness that come seemingly from nowhere. They fly by your head. They take you by surprise. They smell good, they look good, they are sooooo tempting. And then [insert gulping sound here] mmmm, you've eaten it. You couldn't help it. You've resisted as long as possible, and it must be safe by now to take just a small nibble, right?

You've been reserved when he talked about meeting his brother and thought to yourself, "Hmmmm, he must like me." Then he talked about that concert in the spring, and you thought, "Wow, really? He sees us as being still together then?" And then he mentions that house in Kiawah, and you're like, "It's a fact! He's really picturing us together."

And you've crept closer and closer to that delicious, sweet-smelling morsel and before you can stand it any longer, [slurp, gulp, chew, savor, swallow] you say out loud, "Yeah, that sounds great. I can't wait to meet your brother."

And the world stops. And he stares at you. And he thinks to himself, "Whoa, crazy bitch!! Hang on here. I'm WAY not ready for that!! This relationship is moving way too fast. Do I even like spending time with her? She wants to meet my family?? Whoa, she wants to get together in July?? Wait a second, come to think of it, she has a funny, lopsided smile. And when she tosses her hair, you know, I've always thought that seemed kinda fake. And I don't like her laugh. And you know what, I'm quite sure that there is no way I could ever love her. Yeah, you know what, I don't love her, and I never will. Yeah! What the heck. I gotta get out of this. I gotta leave now before she's picking out rings and naming our kids. GET ME OUT OF HERE."

And suddenly, he's not calling you or texting like he used to. And you're starting to get that uncomfortable feeling in the pit of your stomach. "What happened? I haven't heard from him all day. He used to send me little things just to let me know he's thinking of me. I know that I shouldn't call him, but you know what, I'm going to call him. Wait a second, he sounds annoyed, agitated, super busy. Hmm, he says he'll call me back. He doesn't. I should try harder. I'll call him again. No answer.

I'll text him. This is odd. Why do I feel like he's running away from me? We're supposed to go to the beach next week. He said he was excited. He couldn't wait to see me before. What is going on here? Things were going so well. He said that he could really see us together. He said that I was the best thing that ever happened to him. He said that I would get along really well with his sister. He said that he's never laughed so hard as he does with me. I don't know what happened?!

So now you're reading all this about the scraps, and you're thinking, "So does that mean that he didn't mean a single thing that he said?" After all, you weren't the one who went there. He did. You weren't the one who brought up those specifics. He brought them into the equation. You weren't the one who acted like there was a future there. He did. You didn't do a single thing except start to believe him. And now you're out in the cold with your head and heart spinning.

You're going over every single thing he said with a fine-tooth comb. You're running it all by your girlfriends to get their advice. You're playing them his past voice messages to prove you're not crazy.

Okay, so let's back up. Let's talk about the scraps. Why was he throwing them? Here's the thing. He did mean it when he said it. He meant every single thing he said, in the MOMENT he said it. But it was a scrap. Men throw scraps. And they don't do it for the reason you might think.

They don't do it to lead you on. They do it to "try it out." See how it sounds. See how it feels. It's like trying on an overcoat to see how it fits. Testing out the waters. Seeing how the future with this person would look and feel and smell. They mean it in that moment. They really do.

The problem is that those alluring scraps are not indicative of where their feelings lie at that early point in the relationship. They are simply "testing-the-water" scraps that are flung out there to give it a whirl and see how they feel about it. They aren't expecting a reaction from it, because it's not really real. It's all part of the "let's see how this feels" test.

Where the problem comes in is that each time a scrap is flung, it's interpreted (understandably) by the female that the relationship is progressing. That things are moving forward. That they are getting closer and a connection is forming. And all of these things cause the woman to slowly let down her carefully constructed defenses, scrap by scrap, and start to believe that even though it's "sooner than she expected," it must be real.

This time must be different. We're moving at a crazy fast pace because he really, really likes me. And she ignores that warning sign in her belly that things are "too good to be true," and throws caution to the wind and eats that scrap by agreeing with him, and thus making one of his scraps a reality.

And in that moment, it all comes crashing down. His own scraps have freaked him the heck out. His own scraps have become "her idea" and man, he is not ready for that kind of commitment because his feelings for her have not developed to the level that the scrap has taken shape.

Is it his fault? No, he was just testing it out. He was going way beyond where their actual relationship had developed, just to see what it felt like. To see if it would freak him out. To see if he could picture the two of them together.

Is it her fault? No, she was taking it slow. She wasn't buying the scraps at first. She was letting them wash over her. Feeling skeptical. But with every comment, feeling more and more confident. Taking each new offering as a "sign." Believing that each scrap was a step closer and closer to feeling like this one could be the real deal. And when she finally eats one, turning that corner and thinking, "Wow, he really likes me. It's safe to believe him," that's when he freaks out and leaves.

And she is left thinking, "I can't believe this happened again. Every time I start to trust someone, they leave me." And he is thinking, "Man, I don't get it. It's way too early in the relationship, and she wants way more from me than I'm willing to give." Not even recognizing or taking any responsibility for the fact that it was his scrumptious scraps that had lured her into a false sense of reality.

So, what, are we doomed? Are women never able to believe a word a man says? Are men not able to proceed in a relationship without freaking themselves out? No, of course not. Because the good news about the Scrap Theory is that there is a crucial scrap-flinging period that must be recognized and interpreted for what it really is, but after that period passes, the relationship really can start to progress at a normal and foundational level.

I would submit that generally this critical scrap-throwing period tends to last about six to eight weeks.

So, here's how it could look in an ideal situation. A man and a woman meet and start to date. During this initial courtship timeframe, the male has begun to fling his scraps; first at a leisurely rate, and then most likely escalating into a scrap-fest frenzy. The female, knowing wisely now that these are simply scraps, smiles ambiguously and allows them to whiz by her head. Some of them are gently lofted, and others have pointed intensity and bounce boldly off her face.

In each case, she keeps her mouth firmly closed, lets it ricochet off or ducks altogether, and makes vague comments at each one, like, "Hmmm." Or "Maybe." Or, "We'll see." And each time, she deftly changes the subject to something non-scrap-like and most likely scintillating. Crisis averted.

My new-ish friend Jasmine (who had recently been made aware of this scraps theory) had an occasion to put it into practice quite quickly on her second date with a guy she'd met online, with whom she really felt a connection. Out of the blue (on date #2, mind you!) he gazed across the table at her and said, "I think I can see forever with you." To which Jasmine, paused, kept a completely blank expression and slowly drawled out the word, "Interesting."

She felt amazingly "prepared" when he lobbed that whopper her way, and excitedly reported to me that evening about how she did not even sniff at that big ol' crazy scrap. I couldn't have been prouder.

Is this game-playing? Not really. It's just an awareness of the fact that the scraps are to be ignored. The scraps are not meant for consumption. The scraps are an entirely separate part of any real dialogue. They are in fact a one-sided part of the conversation, if you will, not meant to be acknowledged or acted upon. (He may not think so, but believe me, you're not meant to respond in any way.)

The scraps are not indicative of how and where things are going. And the more you ignore the scraps and recognize them for what they are, the more you can actually move forward at a normal pace and start to build a foundation based on your true timeline, your true dating experiences, and your true feelings as they are progressing naturally.

Since you have spent six to eight weeks ducking and dodging and deflecting scraps, it should become quite apparent when the scrap-flinging period has come to an end. You'll know partially because your gut won't be warning you that his comments and actions are coming too soon.

You'll know partly because your actual time spent together has warranted the lovely things he's saying to you. And most of all, you'll know because there is nothing better than the organic progression of a true, solid relationship, and building strong bonds based on moving forward together at the same pace; scrap-free, arm in arm.

4—THE HUMP OF FEAR

So why is there a six- to eight-week time period when the scraps are generally flung? Partly it's because of the "trying it on for size" type ritual like we talked about. But there is a little-known obstacle looming innocently on the horizon of all relationship journeys, just slightly down the path from the happy unsuspecting Traipsers. I've named this colossal beast, The Hump of Fear. And even if you don't eat a single scrap, you have to be aware of this potential for disaster and sidestep it deftly if possible.

To paint the picture, let's go back in time to when I was dating a guy in NYC. Let's just call him Pete (mostly because that's his name.) Everything was going great and we always had the best time together; not a ripple in the waters.

And one night after a romantic "Month-A-Versary" dinner, (completely HIS idea, so I ate the scrap and agreed!) to celebrate our whopping two months of dating, I headed home because I had an audition early the next morning. When I got home, I already had a message on my voicemail from him that went on and on and on about how I was the best thing that had ever happened to him, and he couldn't believe I had come into his life. Blah, blah, you get the idea. Very sweet.

I went to sleep, woke up and started getting ready for my audition, when the phone rang. It was Pete—who then proceeded to break up with me. I kid you not!! No reason, no explanation, and no mention of him professing how I'm the best thing that's ever happened to him the night before!! (I actually saved that message for ages to play for people just to prove to others and myself that I wasn't crazy.) Just an odd, robotic-sounding Pete, saying that it wasn't going to work out. And specifically saying, "I don't love you and I never will." Even though I (of course!) had never brought up "love" in the slightest. It was far too early to talk about that, but clearly in his mind he felt like he had to "be there" already because of his scraps.

As a side note, (because this truly would have made a good sit-com), my audition that morning was for a Gershwin musical, so after I finished getting "broken up with" over the phone, I ironically had to head immediately to midtown in time to sing the Gershwin song "Our Love Is Here to Stay" that I had prepared for that day. Yeah, good times.

But even though I had only gently nibbled at a scrap or two, what ultimately had happened to Pete was that all his scraps had built up into a frenzy, and then all of a sudden, what sets in? FEAR. The brain starts racing ahead and working out various scenarios and telling you all the reasons why something's NOT going to work before you've even begun to give it a chance. That's why it's a Hump. Someone either makes it over the hump, or they hit that wall and go racing backwards.

In dating, people break up with what they have going currently, and run off to start all over again with someone new. It's easy to abandon what they clearly saw the potential with previously, and to seek something else shinier, believing that the next one will work better for them. The scraps all come raining down to haunt them and they feel like they have to make a decision, even though you're not asking for one.

In cases such as these, as a bystander to this, all you can truly do is shake your head and LET THEM GO. They'll eventually realize that the problem lies with them, DEFINITELY not the girlfriend—for Pete's Sake!

5—I ATE THEM BEFORE I KNEW

Now there is a very good chance that you may be having a moment of awful recognition at this point, thinking back on one of your relationships that took a terrible turn, and realizing that there may have been a scrap or two (or six) that you unknowingly swallowed in the early weeks that may have caused the beginning of the end. The question I get asked fairly often is, "Is it too late?" In other words, is there a magical scrap-antidote (let's call it a Scrap-idote) that can undo the horrifying effects of the unintended and premature nibbling?

I'm so sorry to say that I don't have very many encouraging words in this regard. In almost all cases, the damage is already done. If you read about this phenomenon after you ate the scraps and the guy in question vanished, well then brush yourself off, feel positive about this new high-level information that you've gained, and go forth into the next relationship armed with an iron-clad suit of armor against any future incoming morsels. You will never be caught unaware again, and knowledge truly is power in the silent war against the Scrapsters.

But the encouraging news is that in many documented instances, once someone finally learns about the power of the scrap and the red flags for which to look out, their very next relationship in fact often ends up leading to "the one." Even a chronic scrap-eater can be saved.

Let me tell you about my friend Corista. She's a beautiful, confident and successful woman who heads up a department at the hospital. Her fast and furious new relationship with her initially very attentive boyfriend was "going so well!" He was verbally effusive, compliments flowing, texted her non-stop, and wanted to see her almost every night. She was reluctant at first to all his advances, worn down by his fervor, and slowly started to believe that his amazing comments about their future together must be real, though deep-down she knew they seemed very premature for the short amount of time they'd known each other.

She started to believe them, kept saying yes to his wanting to see her almost nightly, said yes to going away together early on, and started to let down her defensive barriers. She saw their whirlwind romance as a sign that he was crazy about her and started to believe that maybe this was the long-awaited perfect relationship. Gulp, slurp, swallow—down went the scraps, and she bought everything he was flinging at her, hook, line and sinker.

Never mind that tiny feeling in her gut that it was too much too soon. Never mind that voice telling her that they hadn't progressed to that point yet with the time they'd spent together. He was saying those things, and acting that way, so it must be true. His feelings must be there. It's okay to let down my defenses and scream it from the rooftops.

This is awesome!!! I have a great man!! I am so happy!! I—errrr, "Hello? Are you out there? Oh, you're busy today? What about tomorrow? Oh, then too? You'll call when you're free?" I haven't gotten any texts from him... Maybe I'll text him.

"Good morning. Hello? Having a good day? What are you up to? Doing anything tonight? Talk tomorrow? We still going to the beach?" Radio silence.

She was on a one-way scrap-infested road to Break-up-ville. She texted me:

Her: OMG! I have to get that book you talked about. I ate the damn scraps again.

Me: Oh no! Not the scraps!!

Her: I totally agree. Are you available to meet for lunch?

Me: Sure, what time?

Her: Polo Grill, 1pm?

Me: Perfect.

Her: Bring an autographed copy!!

Me: Haha, okay. (Though I hadn't written it yet).

I met with her for lunch. She told me the whole story. Yes, there were scraps strewn about left and right, and she ate them up. Scrap eating is fun—while you're doing it. Afterwards, not so much. We had a long talk about it all. And I delivered the bad news. You're DONE. No more texting him. No more giving away your power. If he is coming back, it is not because you're cajoling and being there for him and reaching out. The more you do that, the more he's gone. No amount of you contacting him is going to make him treat you the way he treated you when things were good. It has to come from him. He has to miss it. He has to want it.

You think you can save him and fix him, and you are putting yourself last. What about what you want? What about what's acceptable to you? Is this behavior that he's demonstrating acceptable to you? Because you're teaching him that it is. You're teaching him that it's okay to never call you and to only text you back once in a while with two-word answers. If you were to look at how he was treating you NOW, not how he used to treat you, is this a good relationship? Would this have made you go out with him in the first place?

Stop thinking about how things used to be and look at what you have now. Is this good enough for you? How did you get so lost in all this? How is it okay to try to cater to what he wants, and lose yourself in the equation?

You wouldn't do that at work. You run your department with confidence and success, and you wouldn't put up with this in any way in the workplace. Why is it okay in your relationships? You are not going to text him ever. Do you feel good when you do that? No, you feel worse! Waking up every morning and texting him? Trying to get any tidbit back from him? And when he does, you feel even worse because it's not what you want to hear, and you dragged it out of him anyway? No, that makes you feel terrible.

We finished up our lunch with her new vow to leave him alone and start to make a list of the things that are important to her and how he is failing on that checklist.

The next morning, she texted me:

Her: Good morning! You will be proud of me. I didn't text him this morning, and of course he didn't text me either. Rude awakening, but much needed. I promise I will stay strong and keep you posted.

Fast-forward to several months later. I see a photo of her on Facebook with a handsome man I don't recognize, and the status change that she's "in a relationship." I call her up to catch up and get an update on the story.

She had stopped texting that guy and let him go, breathing through it and essentially reclaiming her dignity that she had unintentionally abandoned. She sat down and took the time to make a list of her non-negotiables. She wanted a husband who adores her. Someone who is faithful. Someone who believes in himself and treats others with respect. Someone who has a great relationship with his mother. "That sh*t matters!" she said. She had laid out for herself and to the universe what she was willing to put up with and what she wasn't.

And lo and behold, about a month later she met someone. It was if he'd stepped off the pages of her list. He was funny, kind, mischievous and smart, and he treated everyone around him with the utmost respect. Their romance was a whirlwind but she resolutely resisted the incoming scraps, and kept her thoughts and actions measured and grounded in reality.

Interestingly, she told me that about six weeks into their relationship, he had hit the dreaded Hump of Fear and broke up with her. He was a widower and was freaking himself out with how wonderful this new relationship was, so he found reasons to talk himself out of it. Corista had remembered all about what I said about the hump, and once again she didn't call or text him. She faced the breakup calmly, and although she was sad, she knew that in no uncertain terms he had to come back on his own volition or not at all. She valued herself above all else.

With that space that he needed, he realized on his own accord the beauty of what he was potentially giving up. He was able to face his fears and guilt head-on surrounding the complicated issue of allowing himself to find love again, and they made it through the hump.

I'm happy to say that that was seven years ago! Today they are happily married and expecting their first daughter at the end of this year. She told me again recently that our conversation at Polo Grill all those years ago had a significant impact on her, and that she thinks of it often. She also told me that she plans to tell her daughter all about it someday and have her read this book, which truly gave me goosebumps. It's a beautiful story of being able to take back your power and go from Scrappiness to Happiness. And that's how it's done.

6—BEYOND THE SCRAPS

At this point in the book, it's important to note that my greater obligation to get the Scraps Theory out to the world has been generally accomplished to the best of my abilities, and I've done my utmost to alert the female gender to the existence and dangers of this phenomenon. So if you were given this book by a concerned friend as a condolence after a breakup, or during the narrow window of time in which you can try to repair the scrappage of a broken courtship, please know that you now have completed the section of the book that was imperative for you to gain the proper knowledge necessary for seamless execution and implementation.

I won't be offended therefore if there are countless people who never grace the remaining pages, knowing that my true message at least has been delivered and received. Certainly, if you're in a hurry to tend to a faltering relationship, I would urge you to move on to more such pressing issues and return to these pages if and when you're in less of a time-crunch.

If you in fact do have the inclination to read on, there may be a few nuggets of wisdom you can gain for future encounters, and lessons to be learned from these experiences and stories. At least one would hope. (One being me, that is.) And so here we go.

7—THE BLUE SHIRT

I'm happy to say that sometimes—and I do mean on the RARE occasion—there is life beyond the scraps. In a few rare cases, caught soon enough, the outcome may in fact be overturned. Therefore, it's again all of our responsibilities to make sure every single friend involved in a recent breakup with an "I don't know what happened" story has a copy of this theory in their hands within 24 to 48 hours. It may not be too late for her if fast action is taken. She still may in fact have a chance to rebalance and recalibrate the relationship.

I'd like to think that somehow, I'm a living example of someone who navigated the "scrapath" with a few bruises but made it out the other side.

I was dating a guy named Jeremy about six months after the famous Pete debacle. Jeremy and I had met on Match.com in New York City. (Isn't it funny how that's one of the only websites in the world where you kind of have to say the "dot com" part or it doesn't sound right?) It was a fairly new site back then, and I think I was one of the first females to sign up! It was definitely a pioneer of its time.

Being on Match.com itself was like having a full-time job, where I used to get about 80 emails a day from people who for the most part couldn't spell "Your purty" properly. Yes, the improper use of the word "you're" WAS a deal-breaker for me—call me crazy.

I had several useful rules for Match, which, don't worry, we'll get to later.

So, Jeremy and I had a fabulous first date over cocktails at a cozy little New York Russian vodka bar in SoHo called Pravda. He mentioned that I'd enjoy meeting his brother, and I cautiously agreed, thinking, "Hmmm, that's interesting!" He enthusiastically scheduled our second date on the books before we'd even left the first one.

He then called me and left a voicemail for me while I was underground on the subway that night, so I already had a message from him saying how much he enjoyed the evening before I ever got home. (Remember, I hadn't figured out or developed the scraps theory yet, so I had no clear path or guidance, unlike you, lucky reader!).

Things were ticking along beautifully, and about six weeks into dating, he invited me to go away with him on a trip to Kiawah Island where his family had a house. We had a wonderful time on our getaway, with scraps-galore that were probably floating up and forming the shape of a unicorn in the sky for all I knew.

Upon returning from our trip, within two weeks he was being more and more distant and "busy at work" and calling me less and less, until one night, walking along Houston Street hand in hand, he promptly dropped my hand and broke up with me, using what I can only imagine was a faxed speech from Pete, because it was pretty much the exact same verbiage. "This isn't going to work. I don't love you and I never will."

Ummm, again?! Love?? At what point, only six weeks into our relationship, had I ever implied that we were supposed to be in love? I was flabbergasted. I don't get it! Things were amazing. How couldn't he see that? We'd had so much fun together. What went wrong? And it all seemed so familiar.

Except in this case, Jeremy reached out the very next day and asked if he could see me. He really seemed to want to understand what went wrong. So, we got together at Blue Smoke where he ordered a plethora of delicious things that I was way too upset to eat, and he said, "I just don't know what happened."

And I said, "I do." And I discussed everything that I truly thought had gone south. That the busier he'd gotten, the more I'd done little nice things for him. That our balance of power shifted, and I'd let it. We talked and talked, and at the end of it all, he walked me to the subway and said, "Well, I'll call you." And I said, "Uh, why? I don't need any more friends. If after everything we just talked about, you don't see the value in trying again, well, that's it, right?" And I got on the subway and just cried all the way home.

And that was it. Or was it? A few weeks later I broke one of my hard and fast rules (don't do this by the way!) and called him. He was at work in a busy restaurant and said, "Oh, hey! So sorry, can I call you back tonight? Listen, it's soooo great to hear from you!" And I said sure, absolutely. Feeling like a million bucks! And he didn't call.

About two weeks later I blatantly squashed all my principles yet again and called one more time. And again, "Oh hey!! It's so wonderful to hear from you! I'm working now but can I call you in a bit? I promise I'll call you back tonight when I get off work!" And I said sure, absolutely. And he didn't call.

And so, I was done. I thought to myself, this could be great, but if he doesn't see it, if he doesn't want it—if he doesn't even think there's something worth exploring then, that's it. It's over. Next!

So, I flung myself into my career and exercising, and generally focusing on me. About two weeks later, I get a phone call from him, asking if I want to have coffee. I still had a blue hoodie of his at my apartment, so I thought, okay fine, I'll be able to give back the hoodie at the very least. (Okay yes, FINE—I was looking forward to seeing him too, you win!)

We set the date for an evening he was supposed to have off from work, and of course I found the perfect "Oh I just threw this old thing on" outfit when in fact it was nothing short of fabulous.

At this point it's important to note that I'd turned into a willowy supermodel. Well, okay, not really, but I'd been back to being super healthy, and I'd lost about 10 pounds and looked kinda good if I do say so myself! (If this becomes a movie, let's just say my character, naturally portrayed by Emma Stone, should suddenly morph into a red-headed Kate Moss at this point in the story. Oh wait, we'd better go ahead and cast Ryan Gosling as Jeremy too, just for good measure.)

So, I had rehearsal that day for a new musical in my fabulous outfit ready to see him that night, and on a break, I checked my phone and had a message from him.

"You're going to kill me, but I have to

work tonight. I'm going to have to reschedule." And I thought to myself the only logical thing that every woman would think: HECK NO, you're going to see me in this outfit if it kills me. So, without calling him back (this was before text messaging too, mind you!) I headed straight to his restaurant at the designated time with a determined gait.

The hostess informed him I'd arrived, and he came running out of the kitchen (did I mention he's a chef?) in a panic, saying "Oh no, didn't you get my message?! I'm so sorry I have to work, and, errrr, wow, you look great!"

And I set my best steely expression and said, "Yes I got your message. Here's your shirt." And he said, "Thanks. (Long glance). You look amazing. Have you lost weight?" And I said again eloquently, "Yup. Here's your shirt." (Awkward pause).

He said, "Well I'll see if I can do Tuesday or Thursday or…" and he started rambling about other times we might be able to get together, and I simply looked at him and said, "What's the point?" He stared at me blankly and in slow motion it seemed, he hugged me goodbye and said, "Well, I'll see you." And I said, "I doubt it."

I walked out bravely, head held high in my hot, well-put-together willowy outfit—and bawled in a cab all the way home.

About a week later, I got a phone call from him. "I've got to see you. I've got to tell you how I feel." So, I thought, well, okay, let's hear this. We get together at a little French café on 6th Avenue, and he proceeds to tell me how much he felt like he made a mistake. "I realize NOW that..." And he went on and on about all the things that just about anyone would most want to hear. It was genuine and lovely, and he definitely seemed to have gone through some major self-reflection.

I sat there listening, taking it all in. At first, I must confess, I purposefully pretended to misunderstand his epiphanies, and kept saying "Oh that's great, that'll really help you for the future," as if it was for the "next girl." And after a few times of this, he blurted out, "No, I mean YOU—us!"

And time stood still for me, as I weighed the terrifying possibility of opening myself up again to him when it had all gone so wrong and allowing a minute amount of hope to creep in that it might in fact be different this time.

I quietly stated, "Listen, I really like you, but I don't need a boyfriend who doesn't call me. I know you're busy. I have no problem with that. But I don't want a boyfriend who goes days without reaching out just to say a quick hi. I certainly don't ask for very much, but these are my non-negotiables. And if I call, even if it's for a second and the kitchen is on fire around you, you have to be happy to hear from me. Even for a split second. If you can't do that, that's totally fine. There's nothing wrong with that. But I'm just letting you know that then you're not the one for me. Because that's what I want and what I deserve."

And then he said something I'll never forget, which is, "I know I lost your confidence. Give me a chance to earn it back."

So, I thought, you know what? Okay. Let's see if we can do this the right way. Without the imbalances, without the lack of communication and without the scraps. Just a real connection. And give him a chance like he's asking, to see if it can rise to the level that I always felt it could.

Since that day, to his credit, as my husband and best friend for the last 16 years, he's never, ever made me feel like his busy career or crazy schedule or anyone or anything is more important than us. Ever. And the same goes for me and the way I treat him.

When it boils down to it, finding and maintaining a balance of power is the key to any long-term relationship. Those pesky scraps can mistakenly throw off the balance when they're given the weight that they don't actually merit, but once a relationship starts to grow organically, there is a true chance to even out the scales. When you're able to find a delicate equilibrium based on mutual respect, it then becomes easier to maintain it going forward, even though there will always be ebbs and flows as things invariably change over time.

People often comment on the "evenness" of us, and I feel like that's primarily due to the fact that we honed in on that balance early on. We clearly respect each other and are proud of each other, but don't compete with each other or view ourselves as above one another. So, there you have it. A rebalancing act and success story for the SCRAPbook for sure.

Be mindful
of the
Balance of Power

8—CLIFF THE MILLIONAIRE

Ah yes, no dating book would be complete without the random story of the millionaire hot guy that vanished into thin air, with very few, if any, lessons to be learned from it. But it's such a fun mysterious tale, it had to be included.

In the Match.com era, before either Pete or Jeremy had come onto the scene, there was Cliff. Cliff the millionaire. Great-looking, charming Cliff, who was the one that gave me hope that Match.com wasn't a total bust after eight months of meeting a sea of "meh."

Prior to meeting Cliff, every Match date whom I'd met for coffee or a drink was perfectly nice and sort of looked like their profile pic and had a decent-ish personality, but the chemistry (at least on my side) was zilch. Zippo! Non-existent. I was beginning to think that maybe meeting someone in that kind of setting took all the romance out of it, and didn't allow any kind of magic to creep on in.

Months and months of going out on just ONE date with people whom I never cared to set eyes on again. Until one day, there was Cliff. He was handsome. He was funny. He was witty. He was charming. And one of my favorite indicators of his quirky character is that his Match.com profile photo was a pic of him clearly cheers-ing champagne glasses with a girl, but it was CROPPED so that it was just him in the photo. Like—a cropped photo of him. With a champagne glass. And he cropped her (and her glass) out.

Are you getting how hilarious that is? Who does that? Cliff the millionaire, that's who. Like, with the undertones of "Yeah, sure, there used to be a girl in my photo that's ripped cleanly down the middle, mid-happy-toast. What of it?" Ha. And THAT photo was the one he selected as his main profile pic. Just classic. Of course, I called him out on it, and we had a good laugh about it. From what you might have gleaned from my personality so far, you don't think I would have let THAT ironic tidbit go by—no, ma'am, not a chance!

So anyway, during our drink it unfolded that he had invented some kind of computer software while he was still in college, and it had made him millions, and all he had to do was update it once a year from home in his pajamas, and everyone bought the new plugins. And more millions were made.

In the middle of our date, he looked down

at his phone and said, "Oh great, Switzerland just bought three nannozannobokanos!" or whatever it was called, which completely escapes me now (nor did I comprehend it back then either).

His millions didn't impress me, nor did his adorable green BMW convertible, which no one really dares to own or drive in Manhattan anyway, but it was finally someone who had a glint in his eye, a spark in his personality and a quirky side smile that said, "Howdy. I'm dangerous."

We had a wonderful date with flowing conversation and tons of laughter, and the time just flew by. Before I knew it, he was whisking me home in his fabulous ride, and hinting that he wanted to come upstairs. "Goodnight!" I said as I traipsed up to my fourth-floor walkup, laughing off his crestfallen expression. Don't worry, I'm not a heartless monster; there was plenty of car-kissing first, and sparks were a'flyin'.

This was the first date I'd had on Match where I actually wanted to have a Round

Two! I was excited and looked forward to his call. Five days passed. Hm, well, I guess he wasn't interested! Too bad. He was really fun. Oh well! Next!

And then—ring, ring—it's Cliff. Yes, five days later he called as if it was just yesterday. "Hi Jules!! I can't wait to see you again!" (Really? How do you define "can't wait?") Me, "Oh sure, yes that would be fun. Let's do it!"

We go out again and have another amazing time. Great conversation, so much laughter, sparks flying. He tells me he's going to Paris for the 4th of July and wants to bring me with him. (How's that for a scrap?!) I politely declined. The funny part was that when I told my Mom that part, expecting her to be horrified, she said, "Are you going to go!? You should!!" Really Mom?

Anyway, a fantastic time, with another drive home, and another longing look to come upstairs. "Not till you call me more!" I said laughing. "Bye!"

Six days pass. I'm thinking, okay, that's fine, oh well. He's a playboy anyway. Ring, ring. "Hi! It's Cliff! Sorry, I was in Vegas with my brother. Can't wait to see you again!" (Am I missing something here?)

Me: "Oh hi! Yeah sure, that would be fun, let's do it." We go out again. Fabulous time. Innuendos, sparks, smart wit, banter, laughter. Once again, he drives me home and wants to come up. "Not till you call me more!" He doesn't.

Four days later he calls again. This time I arrange the details of our date. I have special house seats to "The Producers" which was the hottest show in town at the time. I treated him to dinner first at one of my favorite restaurants in the theatre district, because why not! And let's face it, very few people probably ever offer to pay for things around Cliff the Millionaire. He said he had one of the best times he's ever had, and that no one ever arranged an evening like that for him before. Drove me home and wanted to come up. "Nope, not till you call me more." He laughed again and drove away.

A week passed. At this point I figured it was his normal obligatory timeframe of non-communication. But he didn't call. And more time passed. And he didn't call. And months went by. And I thought, ah well, goodbye to sweet Cliff, the totally-wrong-for-me-but-utterly-charming millionaire.

A few months passed, and I met and dated Pete, so you know how that ended. And around then six months after that as you know, I met Jeremy whom you've heard all about.

So, here's the interesting part of the timeline. Remember how Jeremy broke up with me after six weeks during his Hump of Fear? And I became a willowy supermodel? And I was devoting my time to my work and working out? Well guess what? Cliff called then!! Out of the blue. I. Am. Not. Kidding! I was rehearsing for a show and got back to my dressing room and had a voice message from him and this is what he said, almost word for word:

"Hi Jules, this is Cliff. You probably don't want to hear from me ever again. But I *have* to talk to you. I have to tell you what **transpired***.*" I put that in bold because I don't want you to miss that. He literally said, "I have to tell you what transpired."

Now that's an intriguing word to me. And I thought to myself, "Oh my gosh! This is amazing! I'm finally going to get to hear what happened to the mysterious Cliff! Why he disappeared! No woman ever gets that kind of closure. How awesome! I can't wait to hear what happened." And there may have even been a tiny (scrappy!) part of me that thought to myself, wow, maybe THIS is why Jeremy and I broke up, because I was supposed to date Cliff again.

So, I regaled all the girls in the dressing room with this wild wonderful background story, and they convinced me to not call him back right away (as good girlfriends do). So, I played it cool. I waited a day. I called back and got his voicemail, so I left

DON'T EAT THE SCRAPS

a message. Cool, calm, laid back. "Hey, Cliff, it's Jules. Yeah, it was nice to hear from you. Sure, I remember you. Yeah, sure that would be nice to catch up. Give me a call when you have a chance. Look forward to it. Okay, great, bye."

And then—he never called me back. Ever. The End.

CAN YOU BELIEVE THAT? After all that, I never got to hear why he vanished—because he vanished again. One of the funniest things ever. And the word "transpired" was so deliciously dramatic. It could have been the mob. It could have been that he was secretly married. It could have been that he got eaten by his own nannobannoscrannos.

Now remember, my Match.com days were long before "ghosting" was ever a thing. Today we have Tinder and Bumble, and all sorts of complicated ways to stumble our way to love. When you look up ghosting in the dictionary, there it is now in black and white: "The practice of ending a personal relationship by suddenly and without explanation withdrawing from all communication." Yup, that pretty much sums it up—but kudos to Cliff for once again being ahead of his time. And boy, did he ever do it with charm and flair.

So yes, I'll never know the end of that story. Unless he reads this book. Which he can't because as we discussed, no man can, unfortunately for them and happily for us.

In case you know someone potentially fitting this description, you can perhaps even nonchalantly pass the message along. Cliff the millionaire, are you out there? Because I would really, really love to know what on earth had transpired, if you please. In fact, women everywhere need to know. That would be great, thank you.

9—SOMETIMES CLUES AREN'T CLUES

I was never one of those women who had scrapbooks and charts planning out their dream wedding day when they hadn't even met their spouse-to-be yet. I was looking forward to getting married someday, but I had no internal bridezilla tendencies. In fact, I'd venture to say that even after I'd been dating Jeremy for almost a year, it just wasn't in the forefront of my mind.

Until one beautiful NYC day in October we were wandering around on 5th Avenue, and he said casually, "Oh, let's go in here." And "here" was Tiffany's. And he seemed to know where the engagement ring section was. And we walked through it with him asking me casual questions about which shapes I liked and platinum or gold, etc. And the radar was officially raised! I thought, oh wow, it's really happening, game on.

And thus began the hilarious series of "clues" that seemed to be leading to the complete certainty that he was about to propose.

First, pretty soon after that casual Tiffany's jaunt, we were discussing our Christmas plans. We were going to be spending it in Washington DC, where his brother lived, and my family coincidentally lived in that area as well. His parents were flying in from Scotland and we were all spending the holidays together.

We were talking about Christmas gifts, and he said, "I know what I'm getting you." "Only one thing?" I joked. "I'm getting you a whole bunch!" And he smiled enigmatically and said slowly, "Well—you might really like it." CLUE #1!! Oh my gosh. I might really like it?? Hint, hint. That's got to be the ring?! My goodness how exciting.

A couple weeks later, Jeremy said, "You know what? How about before we all get together at Christmas, you and I just go away together on our own to New Orleans." And I thought AH-HA, CLUE #2! He obviously wants to propose before we get together with everyone. How romantic! "Sounds great," I said.

The day we were leaving for New Orleans, Jeremy and I had already packed and were leaving straight from our respective workplaces. He asked me to call Antoine's, a New Orleans institution, and make a reservation for dinner for one of the nights. Upon calling however, I found out that Antoine's requires men to wear suit jackets.

So I promptly called Jeremy back at work and said, "Oh, sorry, we can't go because you'd need a suit jacket." "Oh, I packed one!" he said. What?? Jeremy hates dressing up, and on our first date basically told me that that button-down was the only time I'd ever see him not in a t-shirt! Which was true. Yet he had PACKED a suit jacket? CLUE #3!!!

A couple of nights later in New Orleans, I remember getting ready for dinner at Antoine's that evening, putting on my makeup in the mirror thinking, this is the night I'm getting engaged! How exciting!!! We had a beautiful dinner that night, and right before dessert Jeremy stuffed his hand in his right pocket, awkwardly stood up and said, "I have to go to the bathroom." CLUE #4!! He never goes to the bathroom during dinner.

Oh my gosh, here we go! He comes back from the bathroom.

"Ready to go?" he says. Oh—okay. We left. The rest of the New Orleans trip came and went. Nothin'. We flew back to NYC.

Christmas time came. Jeremy says, "Hey, how about before we go to my brother's house on Christmas day, we open our presents just with us in the hotel." Me: "Okay, sounds great!" CLUE #5! He wants us to have that private moment before we get together with the family so I can open "the one" present.

Christmas morning comes, and we lay out the wrapped presents for each other. I'm looking for "the one" that he said I might really like, but at this point there were several. I say, "Hey, which is the one that you said I might REALLY like?" And he says with a big smile, "Oh, this one!" I looked. It was rectangular and long and thin. Hmmmm—that's weird. I open it. "Ah, GLOVES! How nice!" (Insert deflated sound here).

Jeremy proudly says, "Remember how you told me you lost your cashmere gloves!?" (I did?) Me: "Ah yes, thank you! I love them!" Wwhah wwhah…

We return to NYC after a lovely glove-filled ring-less Christmas. On a snowy January evening, he calls me at work. "How about we go to Gramercy Tavern tonight?" Gramercy Tavern is quite a posh place, so I said, "Oh wow, well I'm not really dressed for it. I'm just wearing what I wore to work." And he said, "Oh don't worry about it, you look great!" So, I waited for him outside Gramercy Tavern, and I see him coming down the street IN A FULL SUIT AND TIE! CLUE #6!! Dinner in a suit and tie in the middle of the week for no reason? Ding ding ding—this is it!

We had a lovely dinner. And left. Mwah mwah...

I had an operetta tour coming up in March in Florida for a week. Jeremy: "Hey, how about we fly to Orlando for a couple days with just us before your tour, and then you can drive to meet the rest of the cast in Melbourne." Me: "Okay, that sounds fun!"

CLUE #7! Oh, he's definitely going to propose at Disney!

We had a lovely time in Orlando. And left. Mwah mwah.

And finally, drum-roll please, on a random rainy Tuesday in New York City on April 4th, when there wasn't a clue to be found, Jeremy proposed to me at the Union Square Café over a lovely dinner in a non-suit. And the waitress cried. And me too probably. Just a little.

But I just love the story of our non-proposals almost as much if not more than the real thing. Jeremy and I laugh so much when we regale friends with the saga because ultimately, they laugh wisely and say, "Oh, he was just teasing you and stringing you along!!" And he's like, "Um, nope!"

He literally had NO IDEA that any of those GOBS of clues seemed to be undeniable hints to me. Not one single one of those things registered to him as being anything other than face value. That's the sheer beauty of how differently men and women think.

Let's face it, ladies, though I'm sincerely quite sad to admit it due to the marked dearth of poetry and romance of it all, but here it is in a nutshell: Most of the time, much like the fact that scraps aren't true, *clues just aren't clues.*

Don't
assume
that
clues
are
clues

10—NICE GUYS DON'T FINISH LAST

We all know the syndrome that exists when the dangerous "bad guy" seems to be the one who gets your pulse racing, and the "nice guy" somehow doesn't do it for you. We've all fallen victim to this at one point or another, some worse than others. The best thing we can do is to grow out of this phase and realize that actually, nothing quickens the pulse more than someone who treats you with respect and does the laundry.

But it's easy to understand when someone may be still caught in the mode of letting the hot bad guys win. And one such person was my best friend in NYC, Beth. Beth had the particular terrible curse (not!) of looking like Cameron Diaz with a million-dollar smile, and always had men flocking to her. But the ones she liked were the ones who you wouldn't necessarily take home to your Mama.

Through the years, the ups and downs and hot boyfriends and even random B-list celebrities that she dated all fell flat, and left Beth wondering if she would ever find true love. I would often go to the Dive Bar on the upper West Side on Amsterdam Avenue where she was waiting tables and hang out with her while she worked. One particular evening, we met a guy there named Ian. He was cute, funny, witty, smart and worked on movie sets, and he clearly had eyes only for Beth. She flashed her killer smile at him, and we chatted and laughed with him throughout the evening as she worked, and at the end of the night he asked for her number.

I was quite excited for her. "Beth, he's such a NICE GUY! Seems like one of the good ones!" Beth: "Eh. Yeah, I guess."

Their very first date was when he offered to drive her to the airport for an upcoming trip. (Remember this is a big deal in NYC—no one has cars, and no one offers to be nice hahaha). He thoughtfully brought her an egg sandwich and coffee, and even carried her luggage down three flights of stairs! Beth told me that on the drive she turned to look at him and thought to herself that he just didn't match up to the vision she had in her head of her "Forever Person." What? He's adorable. Sigh.

Well needless to say, Ian only got about

three more half-hearted dates, until Beth moved on to more "Not So Nice Guys," and the years went on. I'd met Jeremy at this point, and we'd gotten married in October. For Thanksgiving, we had Beth over for dinner at our apartment in Brooklyn with just the three of us. She stayed the night, and the next morning she just couldn't shake the feeling of being depressed that I was married now, yet she didn't even have a prospect on the horizon.

We were heading back into NYC on the F-train and she was lamenting her single status, when all of a sudden out of the blue I said, "You know, whatever happened to that IAN guy?? He was amazing and you "f***ed up!!" And then it was coincidentally my stop at 49th Street, so I stood up with a bright smile and said, "Bye!" and dramatically exited the train.

Stunned, she watched as the doors closed behind me and thought about what I said as she continued the rest of her way up on the train to 96th Street. She got home, searched through all her things for his long-lost business card, and found it, now almost two YEARS after their ill-fated last dates.

Beth picked up the phone and proceeded to call him, leaving one of those disastrous "Swingers"-movie type rambling messages. "Hi! Ian? I don't know if you remember me, it's Beth. We met at Dive Bar two years ago? Well, I don't know if you're married but—I mean, it's okay if you are, this isn't that kind of a call, but I mean—well, I was just thinking about you and wondering how you're doing and—I mean you don't have to call me back if you don't want but if you're still interested in maybe going out some time, I mean..." You get the idea.

And the best thing that Ian probably did was wait about two painful weeks before he called her back! Poor Beth. But he called her. And he wasn't married. And he did give her another chance. And now they've been married for 14 years with two kids and live in Atlanta. She told me that she truly learned not to get stuck in "what you think you're looking for," and be able to stay open to the unexpected.

And it's all because I said, "You know, whatever happened to that Ian guy!! You f***ed up!" I'm quite proud of this. And you know what? I'm also proud that the nice guy didn't finish last. Because once we get past that phase, we really are ready for the right good guy to appear. It just may take a little tough love from a good friend to figure that out.

11—THE MAGIC PEARL

Once upon a time, 16 years ago, my sister-in-law Natasha and my brother Marc came to visit me in New York City. They had recently gotten married and just returned from their honeymoon. I was single and on Match at the time and had recently had my breakup with Pete, as discussed.

At some point during their stay, she mysteriously drew me aside in the living room and pulled a small box out of her pocket. Inside was a delicate white pearl. "This is a Magic Pearl," she said. Natasha proceeded to tell me that one of her friends had bestowed the Magic Pearl on her after she herself had gotten married. She had told Natasha that with the pearl now in her possession, she would no doubt shortly meet the man of her dreams.

Sure enough, within a couple weeks of receiving the pearl, she met my brother! She held onto the pearl superstitiously until after their honeymoon, but she felt like it was now time to pass it on to me, and thus have it bring me luck as well.

How cool was that?! A Magic Pearl that brings luck and love—I'm in!! I put it in my jewelry box and gave it a loving glance and a stroke every once in a while. About three weeks after the pearl came into my possession, I met Jeremy, and the rest you know. Holy cow, this pearl must really work!!

So, I waited superstitiously until after my honeymoon, and I passed it onto my best friend at the time, Beth, who had still not met the man of her dreams.

And yes, that's the same Beth from "Nice Guys Don't Finish Last" chapter! It was about a month after I gave her the pearl, that we met Ian at the Dive Bar! Now as you know, there were a couple years in there after Beth met Ian until they got married, so although I kept urging Beth to pass along the pearl to another deserving friend, she superstitiously refused to release it from her grasp until she was married and the pearl status was secure. Understandably. But soon after returning from her honeymoon, I requested that Beth bestow the pearl onto one of our good friends, Rachel.

Now admittedly I don't know whether the magic was disrupted because I had put in a request for Beth to give it to Rachel, rather than Beth getting to choose the next recipient, or whether Beth in fact somehow broke the pearl. But nevertheless, our magical streak seemed to come to a crashing halt. Our beautiful and funny friend Rachel, for whatever reason, had several serious boyfriends and almost-engagements and what-ifs and heartbreaks—for the next 14 years! But still, no love of her life.

Of course, Rachel, with her hilarious sense of humor, made countless cracks about hating the useless pearl, but being too terrified understandably to get rid of it! Through several moves to different states, the pearl came with her, and she would glance at it and give it love or curse at it, but she kept it in her possession.

And so it went, until August 2018. I had a great catchup with Rachel on the phone and jokingly inquired about the pearl and its lack of effectiveness. It became clear to me that I had to make a big decision. The pearl had to be replaced.

I mean, certainly she needed to hold onto it, because let's face it, dire things could come from throwing that sucker away when it used to yield such obvious power. But it was clear she needed a suitable replacement.

She was moving again and creating a new one-woman show on a cruise ship and starting a brave new chapter yet again. I thought long and hard about what would be appropriate, and sent her a pretty charm bracelet with colored beads and the tree of life of it, along with this message:

Dearest Rachel,

It may have taken us 14 years to realize that Beth broke the MAGIC PEARL, but the important thing is to recognize it now and rectify the situation, STAT!! Hahaha.

I absolutely LOVED catching up with you on the phone, and yes, we definitely have to do that more!! Congrats so much on your one-woman show—I feel like that's going to be incredible for you with so many adventures to come!

Can't wait to come out and hear you. Good luck with the move, and lots and lots of love!! —Jules

FRONT OF THE CARD:

Rachel's Magical Object

INSIDE PHOTO ON THE CARD:

THE BRACELET AND CHARM I SENT HER:

Two short months later, I see on Facebook a status change from Rachel, "In a relationship." And photos of her looking so happy with a smiling guy named Eric. What?! She never publicly talks about that kind of thing and certainly wouldn't post it because she has so many years of being gun-shy and let down and was basically superstitious about it all falling through. I immediately post on her post "It worked!!?" She responded, "Hahaha, yes it worked."

We had another long catchup in which I found out that she had met this guy through mutual friends and had a true instant connection. And yes, she wears the bracelet often and keeps it in the jewelry box next to the pearl. And of course, thankfully she knew enough to not eat the scraps!

Now at the time of writing this, they have been dating for seven months and are blissfully happy. No engagement yet but I feel like it's imminent. Can't wait for my speech at THAT wedding.

I'll do my best to keep you posted, of course, as to whether they end up happily ever after together, but suffice it to say, I've never seen her so happy in all her life. And I feel quite confident that the magic object has beyond a shadow of a doubt done the trick.

So, the sage moral of this story has several obvious conclusions.

1. Sometimes magical objects work.

2. Sometimes you have to create your own magical objects.

3. Who cares if it's a placebo if it works.

4. Love is worth waiting for.

5. Humor is still everything.

6. Don't give anything to Beth!

Make Your own
Magic

12—ONLINE RULES

After my third breakup with yet another actor/musician (when I declared a moratorium on men who care more about their drum set or fixing their own hair than about me), I decided to check out Match.com in New York City. It was back in 2003 when the platform was relatively new, and from what I remember, I believe at that time women didn't even pay to come onboard and create a profile.

It quickly took on a sort of crazy life of its

own! As I'd mentioned earlier, maybe because it was NYC, I received over 80 emails a day to sift through. It was hilarious and overwhelming, and I set about it with quiet resolve that I was going to make it work for me. Soon I had fallen into some "rules" made up solely by me, so that the wild, wild west (or east, in my case) had some structure.

Jules' Online Rules:

1) **Never spend too long emailing back and forth.** I learned this the hard way when Troy, a seemingly charming guy who was a performer in an off-Broadway performance art show (yes, I had vowed no more performers, but he sort of crept into the mix!), used to write me the most beautiful emails before we'd actually arranged to meet. This was back in the day BEFORE smart phones, so I would run home after a long day of auditions or work to read my emails

and always looked forward to his eloquent, funny, insightful writing. We corresponded fervently back and forth, and I built up in my mind this "closeness" of our connection because his writing was so charismatic and fun!

When I finally got around to meeting him in person a few weeks after having corresponded, he was like watching paint dry! A veritable bump on a log. Maybe even like watching paint dry ON a log. He was so quiet and (okay, I'll say it) boring that I couldn't figure out how on earth this was the same guy who wrote with such verve and wit. No more long emails with people after that. Just "How's Thursday at 3 p.m.?" Haha.

2) **Never meet them for a meal.** I truly never understood those women I knew who wanted to go on Match.com dates just for a free meal. No thank you! When you agree to

dinner with someone, you are STUCK!! There's nothing worse than, right from hello, thinking, *"I could never love you!"* And then having to make small talk throughout the evening and even worse try to extricate yourself afterwards. Definitely just do coffee or drinks!! You can always stay if things go well but do yourself a favor and don't be lured in by a free steak. It's not worth it.

3)   **Always have plans afterwards.** One rule that arose naturally and really worked well was to set a coffee or drink date for 7pm let's say, and then tell the guy AHEAD of time, "Oh, I'm meeting my friend at 9 p.m., so let's meet at 7 p.m." Then you always have an out when you just aren't feeling a connection, and simply remind them, "Oh, sorry, I have to go meet my friend now, but it was so nice to meet you!" Not to mention that it actually is quite nice if

you really do have plans, because then you never go home and feel sorry for yourself. You always have a good friend to tell the story to and laugh it off!

4) **Spelling, spelling, spelling.** Well I'm happy to allow you to dismiss this one if you'd like, but it quickly became one of my rules that if their emails were a travesty in spelling, they just didn't make the cut. As I mentioned, if there are only two words in the email and they're both spelled wrong, like "your purty"—well then, I just thought, I could never love you.

Of course, I would be totally remiss if I didn't mention that my husband Jeremy actually has a few spelling challenges himself, shall we say. So, it's a good thing that his Match.com emails were more along the lines of "How's Thursday" so that I didn't notice till it was too late.

I do remember that when I first asked him what he did, since his profile didn't say, he said "I came to NYC for my fame and fortune," and I thought, "Oh sh**t, he's an actor!" Luckily, I soon found out he was a chef, which wasn't on my forbidden list of vocations. Though it probably should have been, since they're just as complicated as actors if not more so! Ha. But I digress. Back to the rules, I'll generously allow you to strike good spelling off the list if you're so inclined.

5)   **Create Nicknames and Lists.** If your Match.com experience was anything like mine, it actually had started to get rather complicated to remember who I was meeting and what their profession was. I think at one point there were about nine people I was supposed to meet whose names all started with J! Jamie, Jim, Jack, Jessie, Jeremy, John, Jeff, Jordan, Jerry… you get the idea. Hey, don't judge – when

you get 80 emails a day, you'll see that boiling them down to meeting just one to two people a week is pretty good! Spelling, spelling, spelling helps to whittle, but man, it's work.

So, making good lists really helped, along with notes of things they'd said in an email or on the phone. And then my roommates got into the act, and would give them nicknames like "Snaggle" for a guy with a snaggletooth, or "Face Eater," for the guy that I had zero chemistry with and then when I tried to say goodbye he suddenly lunged forward and put his mouth over my nose and chin simultaneously (I'm still recovering.) But yes, nicknames help you keep it all straight, and keep you smiling to boot.

6) **The Five-Week Rule.** I'm not going to lie, no one likes this one. I don't know what to say; I have to put it in here, and I'm not going to apologize for it. Because it's a Jules' Rule and it

WORKS. Ignore this one at your own risk. Wait five weeks before you sleep with them. There, I said it. Freaking out? I promise you, it's better this way. I'm not a prude by any means, but this timeframe is actually scientifically proven (not really, I made that up). Not to mention that this coincides with the crucial scrap-flinging period too, which we've discussed at length. So surely you can appreciate that this is for your own good and for your best chances of a successful navigation timeframe.

Even Beth told me that she waited five weeks after her crazy "Swingers" message after she and Ian got back together after all that time. She told me that as hard as it was and as much as she hated it, she did her very best to follow that darned rule that she had been ignoring for years! Because deep down she somehow knew that this one was too important to screw up.

Now once again, if you're balking at

this idea, I have allowed some very select few friends to "adjust this parameter" to five dates instead of five weeks. Not the same thing by any means, and I don't approve of this insolent behavior as a whole. But at the very least, stick to the number five, and no, that's not five hours. Five weeks is best. Five dates is for the weak. Very, very weak. You know who you are.

So, all in all, Jules' Online Rules are quite simple. I probably should have made 10 of them because let's face it, lists of 10 are just—fabulous. But that's all there is. Not too demanding. Not hard to follow for the most part.

Plus, when you go around asking your friends, "Well, you follow Jules' Rules, don't you?!," which you will hopefully do quite frequently, it'll be easier for you to remember six than 10.

But they all work together as a finely tuned machine to set you up for online success. And for those of you who would "never do online dating" (insert horrified, indignant expression here), you're not excused— Rule #6 applies BOTH online or offline and should be a non-negotiable part of your dating pact to yourself. SCRAPSOLUTELY!

Don't Eat
e Scraps

Follow the Online Rules

13—MINDSET MATTERS

Something happened to me that I would venture to say hasn't happened to anyone reading this book. Or anyone you know. Or anyone THEY know. In fact, it probably has only happened to a handful of people ever. Have you ever been personally booed by 7,000 people? No? No one?

Yes, the experience of being booed by 7,000 people was probably the worst moment of my life, turned into most triumphant days of my life; and certainly, one of the most memorable.

I was 24 years old, and I was "Maria" on the national/international tour of "The Sound of Music" in the US, Canada, and Korea. I toured for a year and half in this role, but then the theatres in Singapore, Bangkok and Hong Kong had thousands and thousands of seats, so the presenters in those countries decided they needed a star. So, they brought on a very well-known public figure to play the role in those countries, and I became her understudy for that part of the Asian tour.

I had spent the whole one and a half years during the tour having to be careful of my singing voice and health, and not staying out late with the cast, so although it was tough to relinquish the lead role in some ways, there was a certain relief in being able to be "just a nun."

As Maria, I used to get to the theatre two hours ahead of time to prepare. As a nun in the ensemble, I got there right at my half-hour call time. As Maria, I would warm up my voice and get into character. As a nun, I would slap on my habit and go!

For two months as a member of the ensemble, I started really relaxing and enjoying my travels to the Asian palaces and sights and may have even enjoyed wild flirtations with the handsome drummer in the orchestra. (That could be another chapter entirely on why you shouldn't date a drummer, but let's leave that one alone.)

On this particular day in Hong Kong, I had gotten to the theatre at half-hour, after a particularly fun day touring around the city. But as I approached, I could see that the theatre presenters and my stage manager were waiting for me at the stage door with panicked expressions. The celebrity playing "Maria" had food poisoning, and I had to go on in the role! I hadn't done the part in over two months since we had closed the show in Korea, and I had never even had a conversation with the guy who was playing "Captain Von Trapp" who had come onboard along with our celebrity when she joined the cast.

They were pacing back and forth frantically and telling me I had to "do well" because everyone could still ask for their money back after they saw the show, since this particular person's name was billed "above the title." As in, *Ms. Super Famous Person* in the "Sound of Music," versus just "The Sound of Music" with *Ms. Super Famous Person*. This makes a difference apparently, and they were very concerned. I promptly told them they needed to leave so that I could go over my lines and see if my costumes still fit!

At 8 p.m., all the nuns are in the wings ready for their initial entrance." "Maria, Maria—where's Maria," they would say, as they cross the stage in front of the curtain, and then the tremolo in the orchestra starts, and the curtain rises to reveal the mountains and Maria lying on a rock, and she begins to sing the title song of the show, *"The hills are alive with the sound of music..."*

I go behind the curtain to assume my position on my rocks, running last minute lines in my head. Suddenly, the voice on the microphone announces, "TONIGHT, the role of Maria will be played by "Julie Lynne Price." (My stage name.) And 7,000 people started to boo.

"BOOOOOOOOOOOOOOOOOOOO!!!!"

Yep. The loudest sound you've ever heard. And then they made the same announcement in Chinese, and they booed even louder.

"BOOOOOOOOOOOOOOOOOOOO!!!!"

I've never heard such a sound in all my life. And every part of me thinks, "I can't believe I have to do this." And then I lie there, thinking, "You know what? I'm going to sing my face off. And I'm going to give them the best performance of my life." I remember so clearly actually thinking the words, "I'm going to WIN."

All the nuns in the wings are nervously eying me with sympathy. The music starts. They do their cross across the stage, "Maria, Maria—where's Maria." The tremolo in the orchestra starts, and the curtain rises to reveal the mountains and me and—WHOOSH!! I can just feel the wall of energy of 7,000 people HATING ME before I'd even opened my mouth.

My 24-year-old self takes a deep breath and starts to sing. And I sing the title song, "The Sound of Music." And the show progresses. I move on to "Do Re Mi." And then "My Favorite Things." And then "The Lonely Goatherd." And finally, little by little—I can feel them coming around. I can feel the energy in the room shifting. I can sense that they are with me in my scenes and in my songs, and as I live the experience of winning over the seven children and falling in love with the Captain and getting married and escaping from the Nazis... and the entire three hour show where I barely leave the stage with 14 costume changes and leave my heart on the floor.

And when I run out for my curtain call, 7,000 people jump to their feet and cheer like a rock concert. For the second time that day, it is a sound like I've never heard before and most likely never will again.

Why am I sharing all this? Well partly because this is one of the most significant experiences in my lifetime, and this is the second book I've written, so if I didn't mention it in this one either then I'd have to write a third book.

But mainly, it's because I am a huge advocate of the power of mindset, mindset, mindset. This is an extreme example of getting booed by thousands of people, but it happened to me at an early age, and I learned a massive life-long lesson from it. I'll never forget making that split decision to win and overcome the adversity facing me. It could have gone so differently if I had crumbled and not believed in myself. If the decision in my head wasn't strong and resolute before I'd even opened my mouth. If I hadn't felt the fear, breathed through it, and done it anyway.

I joke that after that, nothing in life could possibly be as difficult as getting booed by all those people, or even being in the acting profession in general and getting rejected day after day. After that, hey, sales is easy! Relationships? No problem! Nailed it!

But if you're not able to heal your mindset first, no relationships work. If you don't believe in yourself. If you secretly believe you still deserve the bad guy. If you have trouble keeping the balance of power because you consistently put yourself last. If you put up with someone treating you less-than. If you don't care that scraps are just scraps because you're desperate for positive affirmation.

We can blame other people's actions all day long but if you have a negative or self-effacing attitude in life, you will not ever find the happiness you seek. Being in a relationship will not transform you into a positive person. Being in a growth mindset is the only way to be capable of change and resilience, which is imperative for healthy relationships to thrive.

We don't need to go into too much detail because there are a million books written about self-esteem and a positive frame of mind. If you're not good at it, get good. Work hard at it. It comes more naturally to some people than others.

But it's definitely something that you can make improvements in, and it will be the main determining factor of your success overall in achieving happiness and balance. Your "relationship status" before anything else needs to be inner peace, gratitude and self-love. I truly want you to be able to live Scrappily Ever After.

14—THE PERFECT ENDING TO THE PERFECT BOOK

So how does it all end? What does it all mean? Let's pull out the workbook and complete Exercise Seven on how you're going to take immediate action and apply these important concepts to your life today.

But seriously, it is very difficult to even

begin to wrap up a book like this because this topic can never fully be explored, and the concerns can never be fully addressed. I call it the "perfect ending to the perfect book" facetiously, because it's virtually impossible for a message like this to be all things to all people.

Like when the best TV series in the world in season seven suddenly comes to an unsatisfying, crashing halt in the final episode with either maddeningly loose ends or ridiculously tied up in perfect bows, but in reality, let's face it, nothing is going to satisfy you either way, is it?

The good news is that if you still have any lingering questions that weren't covered here, chances are someone else has written about it already, so you can have a sufficient supply of antidotes for your unaddressed ailments. Though be forewarned, their take on it may not be as funny as mine, I'm afraid. I'm just sayin'.

I will say this. Without a doubt, you have been truly one of the best, most insightful readers I've ever had. Naw, that was a scrap, I was just testing you. (How did you do? Did your pulse quicken with the unwarranted random compliment, or did you let it whiz by your head nonchalantly with your mouth firmly locked in a closed position?)

Ultimately this compilation of stories in all their glory has been presented together in one tidy place for the sole purpose of gently conditioning your mind for your interpretations of future events yet to come. The stories are real, they're raw, it's complicated. It all happened. Or at least, this is the way I remember it, and that's what's really important.

Now I have to ask, are you one of those special people who ended up reading this entire book, cover to cover, without having put it down? The number of women who have informed me that they did that was surprising and delightful. I think that's possibly one of my favorite feedback comments to hear (alongside when they say they laughed out loud which is pretty great too). In fact, let's make a club out of it. Who doesn't like a good old-fashioned club!? If you read this book, cover to cover, whether you intended to or not, flying page after flying page, and before you knew it you landed here, bleary-eyed and deliriously chuckling, then I want to hear from you. Just reach out and tell me, "Wahoo, I'm in the *Read About the Scraps All In One Whack Club,* and I'll add you to a secret Facebook group or something. Don't worry, I'll have a better name for it by then.

Now this is the honor system, mind you, so if you put it down at some point and picked it up again later, so sorry. It's too late, and you can't be in the not-so-secret club. Or if you're someone who was informed about the club ahead of time and you gamed the system then shame on you—and them! Your membership is shaky at best.

But yes, hearing that people read it all in one sitting makes me smile because ultimately I think I did want this to feel like a two hour lovely movie, where you have an experience, you relate to some things, you laugh and cry at some things, you maybe even zone out at some points—but all in all you walk away feeling like you've been hugged or forever changed in an almost imperceptible way that you can't quite describe. Yes! That was my wish for this project, alongside my passionate desire to finally get this message out to the world in the hopes that it will help someone. Or a whole bunch of someones.

My friends always joked around that someday I'd be explaining the Scraps Theory to the entire world on "Oprah" as she gently leaned forward and dramatically queried, "Jules—TELL US about the scraps! What do we need to know!?" And then grandly gesturing to the audience, "You get a scrap! And YOU get a scrap! And YOU get a scrap…" Or wait, I think that was a car.

Sadly, now her show has gone off the air (SELFISH!!) so all hope of getting the word out on a larger scale is dashed. Not to mention that I'd have to probably appear in disguise, like Sia, wearing a black and white wig or a lampshade on my head and a voice distorter, to grandly protect my identity from the confused and irate men of the world who are still trying to get their hands on this book.

Well, shoot—there's always Ellen, who, let's face it, would be more likely to get my sense of humor anyway. Not to mention that I have insane tongue tricks that would fascinate her and her audience, but I've always been staunchly determined never to let that be the thing that I'm famous for.

But all kidding aside, it truly does make a difference to have this wry understanding of human behavior in your back pocket and a general awareness on your radar.

Just a couple of weeks ago I was having a coffee catch-up with a great friend, Kaitlyn, who had been verbally apprised of my Scraps Theory an entire year ago, and had moved to Portland, Oregon soon afterwards. She started telling me how much it helped her when she had met a new potential partner. They dated briefly, and she said that the whole time he was throwing scraps and empty "lovebombs" without the true substance behind it.

She told me, "You know, I remembered what you said about not eating the scraps. And I just looked ahead into the future and, I can't explain it, I just clearly recognized the pattern that I always fall into. I keep your theory close to my heart and remember it every time someone promises me the 'moon and more' a little too early on in the relationship."

She said she feels like she saved herself two years of a damaged relationship that her old self would have wound up resenting, because she just recognized it. She just... identified it. And that's the key. Maybe the key to everything.

I was blown away to hear her say how much my one tiny concept helped her to keep perspective and, in her mind, dodge that bullet. All in all, that just simply sums up all that I could have hoped for and more with getting the word out about this in the hopes of helping even just a few.

So, as they say, all good things must come to an end, and so must this story. Although I've never really cared for that expression because, why should it, actually? If you believe you deserve the best and you keep searching for it every day, there's no reason that all good things should have to end.

In fact, did you know that the original expression is actually **"All things must come to an end."** And some jerk added the word "good" in there a long time later, and it stuck.

Yes, it's a fact that all things must end, good or bad, but it's just completely pessimistic to add the word "good" and just focus on that part of it. Whoever did that, kindly step forward and admit your terrible contribution to society's skewed belief system. Probably the same Debbie Downer who declared "Nice guys finish last."

Relationships are, by nature, complicated, but having a greater understanding of yourself and others will always, ALWAYS maximize your chance of success. It will happen with the "right person"—not necessarily just the "right timing."

The right person can even come back if they've gone away, like in my case. Or more than one person has the potential to be the right person. I personally have never believed that there's only just one person out there for everyone. There are zillions of potential connections out there where two souls can find each other and truly feel as if they are seen, heard and valued by the other, which is what true connection is all about.

Always remember there is a big difference between compromising within a relationship (which we all must do) and compromising yourself and the great connection you deserve. Never bend on that part.

Never settle for "good enough." Never

break Jules' Rules. Never date a guy named Pete. Never let a man read this book. Never understudy a celebrity in a Broadway musical. Never read self-help books (unless they're funny). Never let someone eat your face. Never mock someone for braving the world of online dating. Never get mad when your favorite TV binge-series comes to an end. Never give someone gloves instead of an engagement ring. Never stop seeing the humor in life.

And never, just never, ever, ever eat those little tiny scrumptious delectable scraps that are carelessly or meticulously flung your way.

And you'll be just fine.

GLOSSARY

Scrapilicious words for a scrappy new world.

Handiscrapped – Having a condition that markedly restricts one's ability to continue a relationship beyond six to eight weeks

Inscrapnia – The inability to sleep because you can't stop running the recent scraps he flung through your mind and futilely trying to interpret their pointless meaning

Scrapendectomy – The emergency surgical operation to remove the deepest, sharpest scraps lodged ominously throughout the abdomen

Scrapgoat – You, when he blames you for all his wrongdoings and scrap-flinging behavior and pretends you were the one who essentially ruined everything *(as if!!)*

Scrapilicious – Dangerously delectable and lovely—highly pleasant to the tastebuds

Scrapology – A regretful acknowledgement that harmful scraps were in fact swallowed whole, with dire consequences to follow

Scrapparition – A ghostlike image of a scrap in the breeze with the ability to haunt you, long after it's been flung

Scrappauling – Very bad, awful and frightful scraps causing immediate shock or dismay

Scrappa Valley – The beautiful mountainous region famous for where the highest-flung scraps migrate and eventually settle

Scrappetizer – The tiny flying nuggets that generally precede a scrap frenzy

Scrapplicant – The main candidate applying for your affection and approval; generally a cheerful, carefree scrap-thrower until at which point his application is hastily withdrawn due to freaking himself out

Scrappreciate – To recognize the full value of a scrap as to what it is, so as to not take even a sniff

Scrapprehensive – Anxious or fearful that a scrap will be flung at your face at any given moment

Scrapproachable – Friendly and easy to talk to... generally welcoming and strangely agreeable, which leads to letting down your defenses and WHAM! i.e. The *calm before the storm*

Scrappucino – Frothy, delicious, warm scraps that are pressure-steamed into liquid and slide down the throat, typically at the end of a scrap-filled romantic dinner

Scrappy – Bound, determined and full of resolve to apply the scraps theory to your next or current relationship

Scraptitude – The natural ability to fling scraps with reckless abandon and without fear of consequences

Slap-Scrappy – Dazed and stupefied by a series of blows to the head and heart

Telescrapic – Capable of knowing exactly when a scrap is about to get thrown your way; finely-tuned instincts and awareness from all the practice and scraperience

Unscraperoned – Unaccompanied and unsupervised, and left to your own instincts and devices to deal with the scraps alone; a dangerous state of being, without enlightened, well-meaning friends to appropriately guide you along the treacherous path into the light

Wirescrapping – 1) When you make your friend listen to your voicemail messages that he left just to prove you're not crazy after he totally abandons you. 2) Having your friend sit at the next table over, to eavesdrop and gesture wildly to prevent you from eating any tasty morsels that are flung your way

ABOUT THE AUTHOR

Jules Price grew up outside of Washington, D.C. She received a bachelor's degree in psychology and music at Connecticut College, and then moved to New York City to pursue her passion of singing and theatre. She performed professionally for 15 years in musicals and operettas, including the National and International Tour of *The Sound of Music as* "Maria" throughout the U.S., Canada and Korea, and then understudied Marie Osmond in the role throughout Singapore, Bangkok, and Hong Kong. She currently still performs with the New York City Ballet as a principal singer in *West Side Story Suites.*

Jules relocated to Sarasota, Florida with her husband Jeremy, the chef/owner of Innovative Dining, a boutique private dining and catering company. It was there that she was first introduced to an online greeting card and gift business, having received a birthday card and gift card from someone she'd never met. With no previous background in the profession, Jules instantly saw the value of the tool and the exciting opportunity it presented. She moved forward with focus, enthusiasm, and a desire to help and support others. This business opened up an unexpected worldwide platform to voice her down-to-earth and relatable advice and experiences to help others grow their business.

Her inspirational mindset, quirky sense of humor, and ability to empower and inspire people into action has created a wide impact across both business and personal realms. She continues to be a corporate motivational trainer, voiceover artist, top earner in relationship marketing, and author of her first book, *Secrets from the SOC Drawer.* Jules is passionate about helping others to "listen to life," get out of their own way, and achieve all the success they desire.

A Note from Jules:

Hello Wonderful Reader!! I truly hope you've enjoyed reading "Don't Eat the Scraps" and all of Jules' Rules! I would absolutely love to hear your thoughts about it and what parts you resonated with most.

Special Gift: Please visit www.DontEattheScraps.com and enter your email and any comments at the bottom, and you'll receive a FREE BONUS VIDEO MESSAGE from me!

Also, if you loved the book, please consider leaving me a heartfelt review on Amazon.com. I would appreciate that so much. Together we can help so many go from Scrappiness to Happiness!

Jules